E.M. HONEYCUTT ELEMENTARY

# What Happens When
# Food
# Cooks?

# What Happens When

# Food Cooks?

Daphne Butler

RSVP
RAINTREE
STECK-VAUGHN
PUBLISHERS
The Steck-Vaughn Company
Austin, Texas

Published by Raintree Steck-Vaughn Publishers, an imprint of Steck-Vaughn Company

**Library of Congress Cataloging-in-Publication Data**

Butler, Daphne, 1945–
    Food cooks? / Daphne Butler.
        p.    cm. — (What happens when—?)
    Includes index.
    ISBN 0-8172-4155-8
    1. Cookery—Juvenile literature. [1. Cookery. 2. Food.]
    I. Title.  II. Series.  III. Series: Butler, Daphne, 1945– What happens when—?
    TX652.5.B88   1996
    641.5—dc20                           95-13659
                                               CIP
                                             AC

Printed and bound in Singapore
1 2 3 4 5 6 7 8 9 0 99 98 97 96 95

# Contents

11840

# Do You Like to Cook?

Do you help in the kitchen?

What do you like to make most of
all—cookies, apple pie, or do you
have a special favorite?

# Baking

When you make a cake or cookies, you put all the **ingredients** together. They make a creamy mixture.

This mixture is baked in the oven. The heat makes it turn firm and golden brown in color.

Once your cake or cookies have cooled, they are delicious to eat.

Eggs are an important part of a cake.

Eggs start off runny. But they become solid when they are heated. Think about what happens to a boiled egg.

In a cake mixture, the eggs are broken
up. They are spread around with all
of the other ingredients.

When you bake a cake, it becomes
firm—like a cooked omelette.

11

# Bread

We do not always use eggs when we bake. Bread needs flour, water, salt, and **yeast**. These are mixed together to make a **dough**.

The dough rises because yeast gives off bubbles of **carbon dioxide**.

When the bread cooks, the carbon dioxide is trapped inside. This makes bread fluffy and light.

13

11840

# Pastry

Pastry has no eggs or yeast. It is just flour, water, salt, and **shortening**.

When it cooks, it forms a hard crust. It is just right for making apple pie.

The apples inside the pie become soft and sweet as they cook.

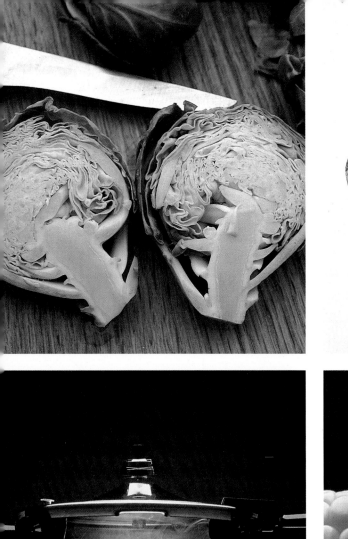

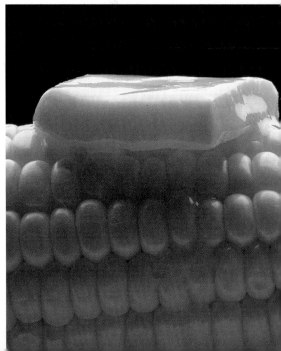

# Vegetables

Uncooked vegetables can be hard to eat. But once they are cooked, they become softer and easier to chew.

Vegetables can be boiled in water or baked in the oven. Can you think of other ways to cook vegetables?

# Meat and Fish

Meat and fish are also easier to eat after they have been cooked.

The cooking softens the meat so that you are able to chew it properly.

Cooking meat and fish also kills
**bacteria**. Bacteria are like germs.
They can make you very sick.

Pasta is made from a flour paste.
The paste is cut into shapes and
then dried. Pasta can be stored for
a long time.

When pasta is cooked in boiling
water, it becomes soft. It is often
eaten with sauce and grated cheese.

# From Beans to Rice

Peas, beans, rice, and many other seeds can be dried and stored.

They are cooked in boiling water until they become soft. They are usually mixed with other foods.

# Jam

Most fruit doesn't need to be cooked. It is delicious to eat just as it is. But it does start to go rotten quickly.

If fruit is boiled with sugar for an hour or so, it turns into jam.

Once it is placed in a sealed jar, jam can be kept for months. This way the fruit can be enjoyed all through the year.

# Preserves

Another way of keeping fruit is to first seal it in jars.

The jars of fruit are then boiled in water for several hours. We call these **preserves**.

The bacteria that make fruit rot are killed. So the sealed jars of fruit can keep for a very long time.

**bacteria** Tiny life forms that are all around us. All harmful bacteria are killed when they are cooked.

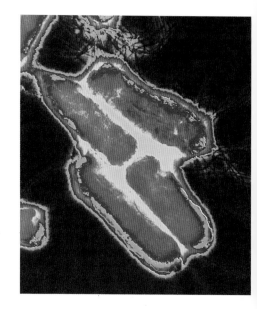

**carbon dioxide** A gas that makes cakes and bread rise. It also makes drinks fizzy.

**dough** A mixture of flour and water that sticks together. It can be worked with the hands like clay.

**ingredients** The parts needed when cooking or baking.

**preserves** Fruits or vegetables that have been heated and sealed in bottles or jars.

**shortening** A type of fat used to make a cake or pastry light or flaky.

**yeast** An ingredient that is used to make bread rise.

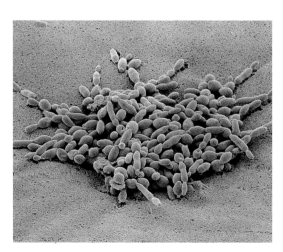

# Index

**M**
meat 18, 19
mixture 8, 11

**O**
omelette 11
oven 8, 17

**P**
pasta 20, 21
pastry 14
peas 22
preserves 27, 29

**R**
rice 22

**S**
sauces 21
shortening 14
sugar 14, 24

**V**
vegetables 17, 18

**W**
water 13, 14, 17, 21,
    22, 27

**Y**
yeast 13, 14, 29

Globe Enterprises © 1993
Published in association with Macdonald Young Books Ltd